The Grief Performance

CLEVELAND STATE UNIVERSITY POETRY CENTER
NEW POETRY

Michael Dumanis, Series Editor

John Bradley, *You Don't Know What You Don't Know*
Lily Brown, *Rust or Go Missing*
Elyse Fenton, *Clamor*
Emily Kendal Frey, *The Grief Performance*
Dora Malech, *Say So*
Shane McCrae, *Mule*
Helena Mesa, *Horse Dance Underwater*
Philip Metres, *To See the Earth*
Zach Savich, *The Firestorm*
Mathias Svalina, *Destruction Myth*
Allison Titus, *Sum of Every Lost Ship*
Liz Waldner, *Trust*
Allison Benis White, *Self-Portrait with Crayon*

For a complete listing of titles please visit
www.csuohio.edu/poetrycenter

The Grief Performance

poems

Emily Kendal Frey

Winner of the 2010 Cleveland State University
Poetry Center First Book Prize

Cleveland State University Poetry Center
Cleveland, Ohio

ISBN 978-1-880834-94-7

First edition

17   16   15   14   13   5   4   3   2

This book is published by the Cleveland State University Poetry Center,
2121 Euclid Avenue, Cleveland, Ohio 44115-2214
www.csuohio.edu/poetrycenter and is distributed by
SPD / Small Press Distribution, Inc. www.spdbooks.org.

Cover image: *Free Radicals* by Sam Weber. Cover design by Amy Freels.

The Grief Performance was designed and typeset by Amy Freels in Stone
Print with Optima display.

LIBRARY OF CONGRESS CATALOGING-IN-PUBLICATION DATA
Frey, Emily Kendal, 1976–
    The grief performance : poems / Emily Kendal Frey.—1st ed.
        p. cm.— (New poetry)
    "Winner of the 2010 Cleveland State University Poetry Center First Book
Prize."
    ISBN 978-1-880834-94-7 (acid-free paper)
    I. Title. II. Series.
    PS3606.R4866G75 2011
    811'.6—DC22

                                                                2010052620

Acknowledgments & Notes

Grateful thanks to the editors of the following publications (in which many of these poems first appeared): *DIAGRAM, Ink Node, Octopus, Oregon Literary Review, Mudlark, RealPoetik, Sixth Finch* and *The Oregonian*.

"Your First Bed," "The End," and "The History of Knives" are for ZS.

"Kelp Forest" is for SD and is enthusiastically borrowed from his deep sea endeavors.

"Falun Dafa" is for JM.

"Love Letter" is for SPH.

"The Train Dreams It Is Flying" is for CT.

"I'm the Scenery" is all EZ.

"Birds Are So Soft" I stole from my dear friend LW and Ms. Peepers, her (former) bird.

"A Meditation on a Meditation of Frost" models its form after and responds entirely to "A Meditation on Frost" by SRS.

Thanks to my family & friends for support & wisdom

Contents

I.

II.

III.

The Grief Performance

I.

The March

1

To be separate
is to be the smallest

bit angry

I'm not reading enough
blogs

I should be more
up to date with people's blogs

2

A rim is the outermost
way of keeping
accurate

Excluding undeliverables

3

Scent is the part
of sight
we can't see

I spent all day
not doing
my hair

A lot of receipts
and decisions
concerning food

4

Trust is considered
in igloo construction
A flag flown
piece by piece by piece
We light out

We make
for the light

5

Division aims
for easy: not easy

A ratio made
while sleeping

I dream my father,
grandmother and aunt
are holding hands down
a steep hill

We're all going
to the same place

Your First Bed

I keep finding your first bed
in the corner of my first bed.

The stars creak open
like doors and scatter

in all directions as if awaiting
a final decision.

What can I say
about the distance?

Here, body inside my body.
Here's a night-blooming cereus,

light attached.

Beach

Wants the heavier shoulder.
Dune grass firing the greenheads forward.

First off the asphalt to yes.
Grouped in wets.
Mark the territory. Skull crushed.

Glass in a hand
of swollen midpoints.
Glass is sand.

Hearts are cards.

We flip like fish. And settle in
for the grief performance.

Kelp Forest

There's a system
of signs

for speaking
when below the surface

A seal might be
staring at you

but there's no way
to hear it

so the person next to you
lets you in

on the secret

Hasp

I am not
as beautiful as that
terrarium

Not as beautiful
as hands
behind glass

I am badly lashed

My job was to stand
in the back
of the truck

To tamp down the black
bark with my hands

In the sun
pants riding
my hips I was
so beautiful

Why did you leave
me open
like that?

Neighbors

Look at them, communicating
as if a whale

wasn't a room
to stand in

I've changed
a tire's

tiny teeth
To steal

To blend
and blue-harbor

They are playing so hard
on their baby

Falun Dafa

There is no
peace

I am eating
a small bad

pizza and I am
not going to stop

but your faces
rake open

and later
on the highway

I make
the sound

that you
prayed

into me

The End

I wake
from the dream

and a deep voice
has pity on me

says It's the end
and I get up

and move
to the blue room

where you stare
at the TV

and you're dead
your face is dead

and I'm dead
as long as I'm in

the room with you
so love becomes

a blue thing
and we shine

The End

The end
conflates

Your heart
a hollow

of blueberry bushes
Oh the soft

attentive
burning

The place
you stake

to burn me in

The End

I put your tomatoes
in the corner

and punch
as red builds

over me
I take the bleeding

cheeks

The End

My mother
and her dead

sister are
watching me

from the end
Come on

flower
they say

and I love
how they call

me flower
so I walk

closer
toward the light

that is them

The End

I miss my beauty
in the field

the long
tree

yelling
palls of hair

my dead
mouth

open
no bird

The End

Oh syrup
your

breath
my hand

still deep
in the end

the sun
a difficult

cusp
we don't

wake up

II.

Love Letter

This letter is not liver-spotted or decaying. Ferns feather this letter. Never
will this letter be referred to as an institution, nor will it endure or persevere.

This letter has lilt. Clearly, this letter lives somewhere lush. It does not
possess charisma, only depth. This letter is not drenched in burgundy hues.

This is the one-hundred-percent tropical letter. Pineapples bruise and drip
inside these words. This letter would not stop for a circus or a snack.

It is not boisterous or benevolent; however, it is breathtaking. Full bloom:
unscented, oiled. Perhaps the tide comes in with this letter. The octopi

and the flaking salt, driftwood wearing seaweed necklaces, dribbling pebbles
and shells. A rocky sunset in this letter. Illicit beach fires. Sunburned thighs.

All the limes split and squeezed, drying on the cutting board. A crow
in the driveway. Indifferent aunts. One plane missed. Hungarian stew.

And then, he couldn't stop the feeling. He missed her pants and hips,
lint between the computer keys, the purr of the electric toothbrush,

how she bent to pull tomatoes from the vine, dig at potatoes, her various
hunchings. Nothing resigned. Their love expanded, like a balloon too

close to flame. He held the burning tip of it between his fingers. Scraped
at the good root of things he knew. He'd buy her a sundress and grow

a mustache. Put a hand to her heaving clavicles, one cracked rib. The morning was a dewy one. She remembered standing in front of him in line, eyes reaching

the same distance. She could smell the sleep on him. He, wondering at the arc between them, the dragonflies low over the water. Soon it would be their turn.

They wait, together, at the head of the line, each of them holding a particular weight, carrying something. They feel it move in their hands.

The Train Dreams It Is Flying

into its competing image: the river. But
the river can move faster and with more
fluidity than it. Both wish to be the most
dark, the blackest. No matter how hard it tries
the train cannot propel itself away
from the frozen water. The scenery snaps
in half and a tree rises up as silhouette,
briefly dividing the machines—
train and river. The train rushes headlong
into whiteness. So this is it,
what speed is. An outline. A broken branch.

I'm the Scenery

My left eye was swollen shut this morning.
I can't feel anything for the town.
That's my memory of Enterprise, Alabama.
I want to take my brother out to the countryside
and I want you to be there.
Mark can read those awful sci-fi books he loves.
Trains will go by at various speeds.

Birds Are So Soft

Birds are so soft.
You can't imagine.
If you rub them the right way—
gentle, not hard, they love it.
They get pin feathers.
New feathers that grow in plasticky sheaths.
You have to break them up with your fingers.
Fabulous. A head massage for the birds.
They coo, close their eyes,
and coo. You'll see.
Another bird or human can do this
with a beak or fingernail.
Remove the sheath. It's heavenly.
They'll melt in your hand. You will see.
You'll have a whole new set of sounds
you can make with your mouth.

Things Were Just As Bad

Things were just as bad as someone said
they would be. There was a goat, and a hill,
and a bad bus driver with a plan. It was the town's
job to absorb the losses, or build a new well.
It was a place wearing cat eyes. A woman
walking by the general store tripped on a stone
that reminded her of her mother's face. It was all
very textured, like a mask that makes your face sweat.

The Storm

You are not a success.
You arrive at this suddenly,
ride it at zip-line speed
and slam into a tree. The tree
is a madrona and peeling. Your childhood
tree. Your not-success
crackles like lightning around you—
so bright and mighty that for a time
you feel blessed.
Stripped, you divide this branch
from that, walk the wet path home,
sit at your desk, eat your apple
of abandonment.

The History of Knives

When I met you we were the shape of salt shakers. I married my dad and threw him in the ocean. I dragged him along the bottom as he filled with salt. I opened my legs and a grasshopper was there. Your first home was a house on stilts with butter dishes. I slept in the shape of what you told me about your house. I met you and we became pigeons under the rafters and held on hard. We became barnacle-shaped butter dishes. I met you and you put me on ice and I froze in the corner of your first bed. Spring was coming and the buds lined up for us to enter. I entered you slow as life. You moved into life with a sleeping porch and a butter dish in the corner and my dad moved. There was a feeling among us of a movie star with sideburns sitting and holding a knife. I could stab the walls of your house. I could bleed on your house and my dad would bleed. My grandfather taught me to swim and also how to bale hay. After the wedding we sat by the lake and he threw a small stone in it. I saw him throw a small stone in the lake. Let's talk about the Fibonacci sequence. Let's talk about the time you walked around your house and I waited in the park with the sun hitting my jaw. A few albino ants scurried through the grass and your neighbor was waiting to watch us walk into the house. I was not there, not walking, no grandfather, no knife. I was sleeping in your first bed with a butter dish, softening in the late spring. Walk up the hill to your old house and sleep and your neck will be a vein for the city and people will buy vintage ashtrays decorated in roses and the city will sleep in the butter-thick night. The city will be a chorus for you and your neck. Your neck sings, and the porch, and the subway rattling by like a knife. You want to get to my neck and I'm a subway station filled with knives. I can sit by you on the subway and smell your boots. My grandfather took the subway in from New Jersey most of his life. He didn't believe in education. He didn't know what pizza tasted like. I can smell your feet. You think I will lie down in the grass but you are someone who eats butter under the slats. There are three dead people in me.

III.

A Meditation on a Meditation of Frost

1

Affection is a dumb dog.
Whoever said that
didn't own
me,
was not
my master.

2

Because you are unkind
to me, you have become
less beautiful.

3

Today is the anniversary
of every other day. Insofar as
no one knows
anything new
about love.

4

"... because I forgot
how soft..."
I heard you say
as you turned me over
like a split white fish,
ribs flapping. The other half
of the sentence lost inside
your other manuscript.

5

Time stops
for no one
or
as the plaque outside
the now closed Martin Luther King, Jr. Elementary School reads
We shall overcome

6

"If you were alone on a desert island
and could only..."
Most questions are intended
to distract us
from their answers.

7

Scientists are now harvesting
seeds to save for when the world
goes dry. No one will eat when
we're stuck to the sides
of canyons, rinsing our hair
in debris.

8

"I'd bring a book on birds...
or a bird."
... maybe a piece
of old-fashioned
silence.

9

Everybody has their own thing
that they yell into a well about

10

A play is only the set
of actors available
that day.

11

Elves, backyard pit barbeque, lilacs,
termites in the backseat:
the sum of it makes a person
want to: lemons, lemons, lemons.

12

Death makes
preliminary
announcements:
I see you.
You're next.

13

Good advice is misused almost as often
as Q-tips:
you've got a grip
but you can't get at
the hot orange mess.

14

Death, my best and most
insincere opponent,
I'm ready for you this time
with fists of sand.

15

Someone in the office drinks too much.
Antiseptic, booze, metallic spearmint tinge,
I follow it
from break room to
cubicle. That was me
in my twenties—up all night,
fucking fucking fucking.

16

"Look.
It's the great wide
whale of heartache,
beached." You don't know
the size of a thing
until it dries up
in front of you.
"What eyes!"

17

"Believe me,
_____ will only hinder
development
slightly." The doctor
and her mother don't see
this as problematic.
As she methodically eats
everything in the candy bowl.

18

"Expectation is a person's belief
in a prevailing order."

19

"Light, the only
living proof of salvation."
Bare bulb, hanging.
Slashes across your
photograph.

20

The BIG clue
is the first dabble
in desire.
If you had to sneak
it and if you keep
sneaking. Love, you know,
isn't a secret. It's the bam bam
catastrophe. Here I come,
with confetti. Just try and
knock me from this moving float.

21

Horror is self-
referential.
Choose Halloween costumes
that bore you shitless.

22

After the funeral his mother and father
stood, swaying, in front
of the crowd, turquoise beads
pinching her throat.
They were temporarily reconciled.
My own mother next to me,
weeping for God knows what.

23

Cowardice is shaped like an axe.
My axe-shaped bed.

24

Because they seemed to have
what you wanted
(jean jackets, porches, un-
complicated lives),
you trembled,
flushed and moist in their
presence, the muscles
of your neck straining
like earthworms
across a very dry sidewalk.

25

Sure, you can get away
with all kinds of lies and fabrications,
some even worthy
at the time.
Then you die
in the big wooden
chest of glory
alone.

26

"Pelagic" is a word
that means "occurring in the open
sea." This will mean nothing
to you
unless you live underwater
with birds.
I've been waiting
for the tiny dot
of your boat on the horizon.
An act of magic.

27

Take me down lightly.
I do not think it goes
all the way.

28

Hello,
big black shiny deep
understudy
of the hole
I'm going to be
if I can't live
up to my current non-potential.
Stay back!
I'm getting good
at faking failure.

29

A river makes
many entrances
in and out of a city.
We're being
made love to, don't you see?
Bend over that bench.

Emily Kendal Frey is the author of the chapbooks *Airport* (Blue Hour, 2009), *Frances* (Poor Claudia, 2010), *The New Planet* (Mindmade Books, 2010), and *Baguette* (Cash Machine, 2013), as well as four chapbook collaborations. She lives in Portland, Oregon, where she hosts The New Privacy reading series.